JOB STACKING

LEVERAGE THE ADVENT OF REMOTE WORK INTO MORE MONEY AND SECURITY

BY

J. ROLF HALTZA

Contents

INTRODUCTION

The chief advantage, and disadvantage, of being a salaried or hourly employee is precisely that you don't get back what you put in. Hour for hour or pay period for pay period, you get paid the same whether you put in 100% or 50% effort. This opens up an interesting possibility, which is the central idea of this book: Why give 100% to one job when you can give 50% to two jobs and get paid double? After all, it is easier to get two low-responsibility jobs than a single high-responsibility one; you'll have an easier time getting hired for, say, two 50k-a-year jobs than a single 100k-a-year job.

Perhaps you've been looking to get a raise? Well, getting a second job that pays half or more of your current salary is easier than trying to actually land, say, a 60% raise with your current employer. Not only is it *easier*, another central premise of this book is that it is also a lot *safer*; we'll see why in a bit.

How is this premise even possible? Given the nature of white-collar office work coupled with the possibilities of remote work, one can actually hold multiple full-time jobs at the same time. Yes, multiple *full-time* jobs, not a full-time job and a side hustle or freelancing; think multiple W2s, not 1099s. I call this idea "job stacking" or "hour-value stacking," because what you will be doing is stacking value on top of the hours you're *already working* instead of adding more hours to your work day pursuing other avenues of income; in other words, stacking jobs on top of each other.

So who is this book for? My background is in software development, so all my experiences and ideas come from that world. However, I'm certain that said ideas can be generalized to white-collar office jobs in general. A good heuristic to gauge if the advice and ideas in this book can be applied to what you do is if you can positively answer the question, "Could I do what I do from home?" If you answered no, then it's going to be hard, but maybe not impossible, for you to apply what is in this book. If you answered yes, then odds are you will be able to comfortably apply what I write about.

If you grasp the possibility of this idea already and don't need an explanation or justification for how it's possible and just want the nitty-gritty details on how to pull it off, you can skip the first section of this book and go straight to Chapter 6. If you don't quite see how it is possible or have some misgivings, then keep reading; all misgivings, and the real nature of employment, are addressed in the first five chapters.

SECTION ONE

THEORY

CHAPTER 1 WHAT IS JOB STACKING?

Let's think of the formally assigned work hours of the day as a kind of "time box" where we put in some effort or work for which we are compensated:

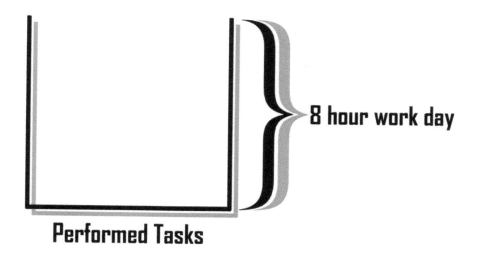

Empty time box

Most of us get paid by the hour, and we do spend a good amount of our paid time—more than a third, by some estimates—doing work-related things. But most of that time, the other two-thirds or so, is spent in other ways; many of us put up a facade, pretending to be working in order to not look bad, or stretch the tasks we have to accomplish so that they take up more time than they should. The reason for doing this is obvious: we simply *don't get paid* for tasks completed but rather for "working hours." The "time box" in this case will look something like this:

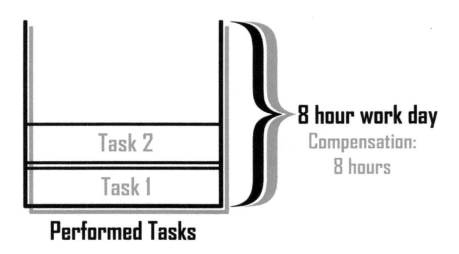

Task 2

Task 1

Performed Tasks

8 hour work day
Compensation:
8 hours

"Underachiever" or regular-person time box

Others—those eager to shine—realize the work they're assigned is not enough to fill their "box" and actually start asking for more work to be headed their way to show off how capable, productive and reliable they are. The reason people do this is to be promoted, to get a raise and maybe recognition within the organization (or maybe simply because they enjoy being busy). The time box in this case will look like this:

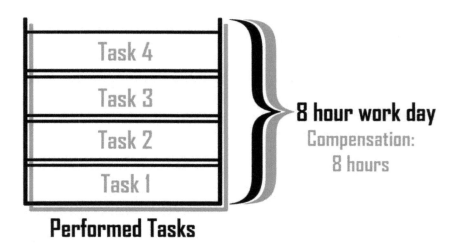

Task 4

Task 3

Task 2

Task 1

Performed Tasks

8 hour work day
Compensation:
8 hours

"Overachiever" time box

Both cases expose a fundamental flaw in modern work, in its philosophy and compensation scheme: **it doesn't actually matter how much you work—you get paid for 8 hours, and if you want more money, you have to jump through hoops within the company to prove your worth**.

Both cases also show a loss of potential: the "underachiever" is leaving a lot of money on the table by wasting his time and the "overachiever" is investing a lot of time and effort thinking it will translate into either more job security or money (even if they just genuinely like being busy, by being busy for only one employer they too are leaving potential money on the table). This loss of potential is what job stacking addresses.

Job stacking, to put it simply, means filling your time box with tasks from multiple jobs at the same time *within the allotted eight-hour workday*. If one job does not fill your daily time box, then instead of either leaving it empty or filling it to the brim while getting paid the same—or a bit more—why not get paid for 16 or even 24 "hours"?

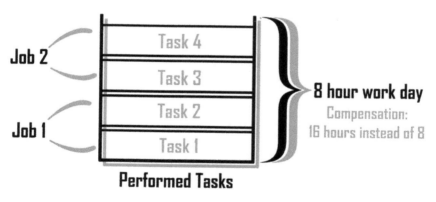

Time box with job stacking

Why should you try job stacking and not freelancing or having a "side hustle"?

You've already done what it takes to get the job you have, you already know how to get jobs like it, you already know what interviews or "auditions" are like and you also have an idea of what the job itself entails. Do you know how to get a "side hustle"; do you even know where to start? Do you know anything about things like marketing, customer acquisition, onboarding and the like? If you do, great, maybe a side hustle is more for you; if you don't, then forget about it—this is all about leveraging everything you *already* know and do, and simply stacking something similar on top of it to make more money and increase your job security.

Job stacking is not about working more hours in your free time on a side hustle, nor about freelancing and getting "multiple clients," but about adding value to each hour you spend "at work" by simply adding full-time jobs—jobs you already know how to handle—to the day.

Job stacking actually solves the issues facing both freelancing and regular full-time employment.

The benefits of freelancing come from you not being beholden to one employer, therefore having more freedom and in theory more security since there is not a single point of failure where you lose all of your income. However, freelancing has one big problem: No clients or, more importantly, no work from clients, equals no money. Sometimes even having clients and work from them still means no money—at least for a while—since they don't always pay on time. Then consider that building a portfolio of trusted clients that give you steady work takes a lot of time and effort.

It should be obvious that freelancing is actually not that liberating, nor appealing, to a lot of people; most people prefer the boredom of steady full-time employment where no matter how little work they get assigned they always get the same paycheck at the end of the pay period. Freelancing is volatile and unsafe; full time employment is consistent and safe—except that that's not true either, because if you lose your only job you're out of a paycheck for who knows how long. Full-time employment may give the impression of safety, but it comes with a lot of hidden risks.

Job stacking then is not only about making more money but, as we will see in Chapter 3, is also about solving the safety issues related to both pure freelancing and full-time employment.

For now, let's continue on to Chapter 2 where we'll explore the true nature of employment in the modern era and why it makes job stacking possible.

CHAPTER 2 How is Job Stacking Possible?

As we mentioned in the last chapter, odds are you don't spend most of your working hours fully engaged in productive work. According to the Bureau of Labor Statistics, Americans spend an average of 8.8 hours at work everyday, but this number is deceptive and doesn't give the full picture; research shows that the average worker is actually only productive for around 3 hours each day. Most of the day, then, is spent reading news, browsing social media or simply talking with coworkers about things unrelated to work.

That is a lot of unproductive time employers are paying for. Why? Well, you might think you were hired to perform some work that the company needs to have done, and that's partly true, but ask yourself: Why would the business pay for a full-time employee when the work that is needed doesn't actually take the "full time"? Wouldn't it be cheaper to simply hire contractors or consultants and have them do the work piece by piece? Indeed it would, so why do businesses mostly hire employees and only have a handful of—if any—contractors? The reason is because you as an employee are not simply hired to do your job or whatever you think your job is; you are hired because of something else you provide to the company. Let me explain.

From the point of view of the business, contractors are unreliable. They have multiple clients and no particular loyalty to any of them, especially if they are good at what they do; you simply can't guarantee that the contractor will be around when you need him. The business might suddenly need a contractor they usually hire, and the work needs to be done *right now*, but since he is independent and has other customers he might already have other work lined up and may not be **available** right when the business needs him. But if that contractor were an employee, *if only* he were an employee, then there's no possible way he would not be **available** because an employee owes all of his time to the company he works for. Employees are almost by definition **available** whenever the business needs them.

So you see, you are not actually being paid to do your work, you are being paid to be **available**, whether or not there's any work to be done—and whether or not that work actually needs 40 hours a week. You are hired because the company needs to have some sort of security that whenever work actually needs to be done, they have a pool of people ready at a moment's notice. This is why you don't actually spend your 8 hours working, yet can't "go home" when there's nothing to do.

It used to be that there was nothing to do about this "dead time" at work; twenty or even ten years ago you had to endure it because you worked at an office with security cameras and the prying eyes of your coworkers, but now with the advent and rising popularity of remote work we are no longer "in" the office, we no longer have the eyes of our coworkers on us, and we can therefore do many things that weren't possible before, like stacking multiple full-time jobs.

Job stacking is possible precisely because the "dead time" that used to belong to your employer can now belong to you, and you can use it to earn more money and have better job security instead of reading news articles or watching YouTube. Job stacking is about exploiting the "dead" or waiting times—times when there is little or no work—of multiple full-time jobs. If you spend most of your work time "waiting" for work or stretching out whatever task you are doing to make it look like it lasts 8 hours, why not make that time **more productive for you** by multiplying your salary? You do this by learning how to manage potential conflicts or overlap between your different jobs (for instance meetings), how to handle expectations, how to *seem* available, and lastly how to manage your tasks when it's finally time to do some actual work.

CHAPTER 3 THE BENEFITS OF JOB STACKING

Work has changed. In *The End of Loyalty*, Rick Wartzman details what happened to the job market by looking at the transformation of four major US companies: Kodak, Coca-Cola, GM and GE. It used to be that companies had some investment in their employees; they tried to gain employee loyalty by providing them with job security and many perks to those that stayed with them long-term.

Back in the day it made sense to try to climb the corporate ladder since not only were there plenty of opportunities provided to do so, there were also tangible benefits. But as Wartzman tells us, corporate culture today has elevated shareholders above employees, so those days of being loyal and slowly climbing the ladder are gone. Yet companies still want you, the employee, to be loyal without them actually doing anything substantial to earn that loyalty—all they have are psychological tricks and speeches: If you've ever been told about "ownership," "owning what you do" or about how you are part of a "family" for being an employee then you already know what tricks I'm talking about. Pair this with the fact that most work is boring, uninteresting or plain useless—what David Graeber calls "bullshit jobs"—then it's no surprise that according to Gallup 85% of employees are not engaged with their workplace, 85% only doing the minimum.

Now, from the point of view of companies this all looks pretty bad and indeed it is pretty bad for them, but it can be great news for us because it means that if we are able to survive at a job doing the bare minimum, then there's room to do much more during the day if we choose to. If there is no point in being loyal or trying to climb the ladder at your job, then you are free to do something else, something better. We can't do anything about the nature of modern work or about companies valuing shareholders above employees, but given those facts, we *can* simply do what's best for us and not what's best for them. What's best for you is having more money and more job security and this is precisely what job stacking addresses.

More money

With jobs it tends to be that to be paid more you need to be "valued" more by the company, and this usually means having to shoulder increasingly more responsibilities. Gaining more responsibility gets you (in theory) more money but also gets you a lot more stress and less time; it also increases your level of visibility so that if something goes wrong, your neckline displays more prominently to the guys sharpening the corporate axe. We already saw how little sense it makes to climb the ladder given the disloyal nature of modern companies today; however, if you *don't* make some attempt to climb, to increase your responsibilities and get "promoted," you simply don't stand to make much more money. How do we make more money *without* increasing our visibility or responsibility? By job stacking, of course!

It is easier to get a second job that pays 60% of what you already make than to get a 60% raise at your current job by climbing the ladder. This is the main monetary benefit of job stacking. Don't be a "good employee," don't try to get more responsibilities or "advance" in your career at a single job—it's not worth it. Get more money by stacking jobs and stay low-responsibility and low-visibility.

Job security

One of nature's oldest and most reliable safety mechanisms is redundancy. With redundancy we create a means of compensation for if something should go wrong; we have two lungs, two kidneys, two eyes, two hands, et cetera, because in case one of them fails or is destroyed it doesn't spell doom for the organism. Humans also apply redundancy as a safety mechanism in our commercial and industrial endeavours: For instance, commercial planes have two engines even though they only need one to actually fly; we also put two pilots in the cockpit so in case something happens to one of them the plane doesn't crash for lack of a pilot. We can also think of savings as a kind of redundancy, since we are overcompensating during the good times of having surplus money in order to take care of ourselves during the bad times of having no money. Similarly, saving some portion of harvested grain, to avoid starving during times of famine, used to be a common practice in the past.

So why would you have a central point of failure for the way you put food on the table by having only one source of income? If you only have one job, one source of income, then if something happens to it, you are screwed unless and until you can find another. This is why the idea of losing your job is so scary and why so many people put up with jobs they hate. Having a single source of income makes you fragile, makes you totally dependent on your employer.

One of the main benefits of job stacking is that we are able to apply redundancy to provide income *and* job safety by making your income come from more than one source, therefore taking you from being fragile and dependent to being more independent and robust. It's a way for you to regain some power and agency and stop being at the mercy of your boss or of a single company.

Comparing job stacking to common alternatives

Job stacking vs. 100% freelancing/consulting

Job stacking is similar to freelancing or consulting in the sense that we are trying to remove the fragility of having only one source of income. Freelancing and consulting, though, come with certain other downsides that are inherent to them and can't be avoided, but that aren't a problem if we stack jobs.

The main issue with freelancing is that it is simply not true that it necessarily solves the "one source of income" problem! I know plenty of freelancers that have only one single client and if that client does not give them any tasks they are screwed. They are arguably even less secure than they would be as hourly or salaried employees. Now a mature freelancer with a developed portfolio and a steady stream of clients and work is indeed in a much safer position than an employee, but if you are reading this book, you are probably not a "mature freelancer," you are someone that is trapped in the world of employment.

Freelancing also allegedly offers freedom, but I have never met a freelancer who was actually "free"; they either had the "one client" problem, in which case they were worse off than an employee, or they had the opposite problem of having too much work, and since unlike employees they truly are paid for results, that meant they didn't have a lot of free time. The alleged freedom that freelancers have is that they can set their own hours, but this is also mostly untrue or true only for a few. A lot of freelancers or consultants are required to be available for specific hours of the day while working on a project, and they often need to cooperate with other freelancers or a client company's regular employees and this severely limits how to manage hours. Besides, not all jobs are conducive to freelance work; there are some lines of work for which freelancing simply does not exist. And oftentimes and in a lot of places freelancers have fewer legal protections than employees.

The truth is, the freelancing world is hard, not actually safe *or* that much freer, and the only clear upside it has over being an employee is that it is more robust in the long term *if* you keep at it.

Job stacking solves the central problem of being a full-time employee (only having one source of income) while offering none of the problems that come with freelancing. With job stacking, you are still paid whether your employers have work for you to do or not, so you need not worry about your income decreasing for lack of work; you also have access to all the benefits employees are legally entitled to (or at least conventionally offered), like reduced tax burdens, health insurance, and retirement programs. Job stacking has all the benefits of freelancing without any of its problems, plus all the benefits of employment that are missing in freelancing.

Job stacking vs. job + side hustle

A popular combination these days is to have a full-time job while also working at some sort of part-time job or "side hustle." This combination is also a response to the fragility of full-time employment in the long term and is in some ways a precursor to job stacking, but with the advent of remote work it makes little sense to have a "side job" when you can have more than one full-time job.

The biggest issue with having a side hustle is not only that it can lead to burnout since you are working a lot more than 8 hours a day, but also that the types of "side jobs" one can get tend not to be very good in terms of pay or security. Job stacking, while being similar in principle to having a side hustle, presents none of those issues and offers better rewards.

The main reasons people still go for the side job are that they either don't know about or haven't considered job stacking or they don't think it can be pulled off. This book is meant to show you not only that it's possible but also how to do it.

Job stacking vs. starting your own business

Many people, myself included, have tried to get out of being an employee by starting a business of their own to see if they can make it big, see if they can become the boss. Unfortunately the reality is that most businesses fail. New businesses have an astoundingly high failure rate. Fundera reports that 20% of small businesses fail in their first year, 30% in their second year, and 50% of small businesses fail after five years in business. Finally, 70% of small businesses will have failed by their 10th year in business.

So while I certainly admire the spirit of trying to start a business, it sometimes leads to ruin, and often it simply leads to being an employee again. It's a very risky move for people with families that depend on them.

Job stacking is safer, and while it certainly doesn't give you freedom from being employed in the short term, it certainly allows you to have more money at the end of each month, which could eventually get you the freedom you want in the long term.

CHAPTER 4 IS JOB STACKING ETHICAL? IS IT LEGAL?

Regular people are being besieged and having their livelihoods threatened on all sides by things like automation or the gig economy. Experts tell you things like "average is over," that you will have to invent your own job if you are to even have one in the future. You get told that a job is not just a job but that you must "love what you do," that you must be in constant "learning" and "reinvention" mode, that you must have passion for what you do, in essence that you must derive meaning in your life from your work as if you were saving the world.

But we're not saving the world with our work; we do menial labor. The truth is, we all just need a paycheck; the meaning of our life we'll find or provide ourselves in Church, family or whatever it is we truly value, not in being some careerist wage slave.

Employers demand you love and be passionate about your job and that you be loyal to the company, but the company can easily fire you to appease some anonymous rich investors that demand more profits. Companies don't care about you and will pull all kinds of tricks to try to squeeze as much value out of you as they can. Why can't we do the same to them? Do to them what they do to us: squeeze as much value out of them as you can and treat them as dispensable and replaceable.

You may be wondering, "If you hate your job so much, why don't you just quit instead of doing all this complicated job stacking stuff?"—a valid albeit naive question. The idea that you can just "quit your job" assumes we employees have the freedom to simply do so, but that is often not the case. Employees have no actual freedom; quitting some job because we're unhappy is unthinkable to many who have to support a family or have debts to pay. Remember, only

15% of people are engaged at work; that means the other 85% are enduring it. If quitting and finding another, better job was easy, you'd expect less lopsided numbers on engagement.

The truth is, if you follow the standard employment model, you have very little to no freedom to choose employers, very little freedom to simply quit your job and do something else; all the power of choice rests with employers. When was the last time you walked into a company and told them *you* chose *them* as your employer and to please have HR fill out the necessary paperwork because you're starting on Monday? It's you who has to prove yourself to your prospective employer in an audition called a "job interview." Companies are the ones that get sent dozens of resumes for a single position; they are the ones doing the choosing. Even when companies are "actively recruiting," all they're really doing is reaching out to someone and telling that person that the company thinks they would do well in their audition process. There are seven billion people on the planet, do you think there are more than seven billion *jobs* on the planet? You are not doing the choosing; you are not free.

In short: we have been screwed, the system is stacked against us and in favor of employers, so we are absolutely justified in trying to better our condition by selectively breaking or ignoring rules and standards companies unilaterally establish in their favor, rules like "you can only work for *us* at any given time."

We will not be hurting any companies with job stacking—in fact a central premise of job stacking is continuing to do satisfactory work for employers in order to stay employed. If the point were to hurt your performance in a way that risked you being terminated, it would no longer be job stacking. Job stacking is not about misusing confidential information to extort or damage employers; this is not a quest for revenge in which we are trying to destroy our "oppressors," we are simply ignoring dumb unilateral rules that companies establish in a total overreach of control over our lives: namely that we can only work for them exclusively at any given time, that they fully own us and our time, or that what's a problem for them should be a problem for us.

Is it legal?

Depends on what country you live in. My lawyers tell me that in the US there are no legal problems with having multiple W2s or having more than one job, and that breaking a clause from a private contract or not abiding by it does not necessarily constitute an illegal act; you could be sued in civil court, but it is not criminal. State law may vary in nuance regarding other things, however, like how many hours an employee can work and therefore bill per week, so please consult with a lawyer on your own just in case.

This is not legal advice, so please make sure you are clear on the legality of engaging in job stacking wherever it is you reside and consult a lawyer about it. I do not advocate breaking the law or doing anything illegal to pursue job stacking.

SECTION TWO

PRACTICE

CHAPTER 5 GETTING STARTED WITH JOB STACKING

We have already seen what job stacking is about, how it's possible, its benefits and some ethical and legal considerations—now it's time to actually get started and do it.

Before we actually get to the nitty gritty implementation details we need to work on our psychological outlook on productivity and dispel some pervasive myths surrounding it. We need to understand the traps of commitment and productivity in modern employment and how to stop falling for them by embracing our right to be mediocre—the goal is to become what I call the "King of Mediocrity" (more on that later).

The Trap of Commitment

Back in the days of IBM dominance there was such a thing as "lifetime employment." Being tied, or "married," to a job and company made sense; the commitment from both parties was there, at least nominally. But lifetime employment and job security died an undignified death and all we have now is job insecurity. But companies, being entitled and greedy, decided they owed no loyalty to their employees, while still demanding their employees be loyal to them. It's like getting all the downside and none of the upside of being married: you get all the responsibility of being a spouse but no commitment, no companionship in harsh times, etc. All you get is court-mandated "intercourse" once a month via a paycheck.

Companies try to induce loyalty with the good ol' carrot and stick.

The carrot comes in two forms. The first are all the psychological tricks used to create "meaning" or "community": pizza parties, arcade cabinets in the office, "free" breakfast, Super

Smash Bros. tournaments, employee of the month, all the talk about "ownership," "owning your work." They want to make you think you're more than just a number on their balance sheet, that you're part of the family.

The second one is what "greatest writer alive" and commentator on modern employment, Paul Skallas, identifies as the game of "loving what you do." Skallas points out that, since modern employees are not only not getting rich, but work and life conditions are such that they can't even conceive or think about building real wealth, the game is then changed, from one of increasing your wealth or bettering your material conditions to a loftier, more abstract one of "loving what you do." If you love what you do then it doesn't matter if you're not getting rich or are underappreciated and overworked; you're still winning in life somehow.

The stick also comes in two forms. First are all those NDAs, non-competes and dozens of other documents and contracts they make you sign in order to guarantee *your* destruction if you were ever to do something "disloyal," and/or guarantee that you couldn't destroy *them* if they pulled something nasty on you. The other form of the stick comes from reputation destruction. It's not that companies go out of their way to destroy a worker's reputation, and I'd say that rarely happens, but the issue is that on your resume, you need to have shown "loyalty" to a company in order to be attractive to other companies who might hire you.

So it is of the utmost importance that you stop thinking of your job as a "commitment," or that you need to "love" it. Your job is not like a wife—hell, it's not even like a steady girlfriend. You need to think of jobs as mistresses that you frequent without being committed to any one of them. You are there for one thing and they are there for one thing; don't make their problems your problems, don't fall for them telling you you are their "special guy." No employee of theirs is special or irreplaceable, so do not ever think to yourself that you owe them anything because they've been so nice to you, and especially don't ever think they feel anything deep or special for you. **You should not feel bad**

about not being loyal or committed, and you should not feel bad about breaking one-sided rules the company makes up.

Keep in mind, though, that there is a reason I do not use the more sordid words "whore" or "hooker" to refer to companies or jobs; I use "mistress," a word that has a more dignified connotation than the other two (maybe "concubine" could apply as well). Why? Remember, companies are entitled and arrogant; they don't see themselves as cheap whores or meat grinders, they see themselves as valuable. They're not there just to make money, they're "making a difference" and "empowering people to follow their dreams." Even if it is a meat grinder they'll maintain a ceremonial and dignified audition/interview process. It is therefore wise to play the flattery game, keep all the dirty business going on underneath hidden and implicit, never explicit; they want you to tell them and show them you're their loyal champion and you will oblige in making them think that you are, but of course in reality you'll be pursuing your own advantage.

The Trap of Productivity

The Trap of Productivity has a long history since it sits at the core of employee/employer relations. The issue with productivity is that there is an inherent and perpetual conflict between employee and employer; the employer naturally wants the employee to be as productive as possible while paying him as little as possible, while the employee naturally wishes the opposite, to be paid as much as possible for doing as little as possible.

In the past this conflict used to be clear to everyone because what employers demanded was explicit and conspicuous: either work sixteen hours at the factory in terrible conditions, or simply starve to death. The labor movements of the 19th and 20th centuries won many battles on behalf of labor (employees) and limited many of the explicit conditions and demands that employers could place on employees.

The conflict never actually went away, of course, and employers still desire to extract as much production as possible from their employees; alas, they can't do it explicitly anymore, since they are limited by labor laws (even if in many places there is no longer any real labor movement to speak of). But there's a loophole. The law only stops the employer from exploiting its employees; however, if employees were to exploit *themselves*, the company would not be as clearly liable. So this is exactly what companies went for: they laid out a trap of creating work environments and narratives of productivity that would tacitly push employees to give more of themselves to their employers, to self-exploit.

Hence why you constantly hear that you should strive to be better at your job each day, that you should push yourself towards "excellence," towards "mastery," towards increasing your productivity. Self-improvement gurus of all stripes and colors are coming up with methodologies and approaches all the time so that you can become "better," a better slave. We've all seen the motivational posts and videos on LinkedIn—the most despicable social media site of all—of people signaling to everyone how they are committed to improving their value for their employer, how they did or built something "amazing," or how they transformed their lives by waking up at 5am.

The quintessential "Trap of Productivity" LinkedIn Post.
Taken from @CrapOnLinkedIn

Self-exploitation is always praised and rewarded.
Taken from @CrapOnLinkedIn

Companies are committed to their profits, not their employees. It's only fair that you be the same way. Be committed to and productive for *your own* projects, profits or income, not some employer's.

Commitment and love should go to those who appreciate it, not to those who simply expect or demand it, much less to those who want to trick you into giving your best for them when they don't give their best for you. Don't fall into their traps: the "free" perks, the awards, the fake social engagement. They are all just tricks to get more out of you. Be excellent in your own pursuits and committed to your own projects; as for the rest, you have a right to simply be "mediocre" at work, a right to simply earn a living by doing "enough."

The right to be mediocre

Yes, that's right, this book defends and advocates that dreaded word in today's world: mediocrity. Most of us are mediocre—average—yet our leaders and people in power hate regular people, they despise the average, and are always trying to make us feel bad for not being on some journey of constant self-improvement. Some people just want to wake up late in the morning or spend their time grilling burgers; we don't all have to become the next Elon Musk, Jeff Bezos or Jocko Willink.

The right to be mediocre is a sort of rebellion against managers. Managers are the worst type of employee because a manager is someone that behaves as if he had ownership of the business when he doesn't, and as such he is a sort of "class traitor," an employee that is there to represent the company and the owner class's interests, betraying the interests of the employees. They have taken increased responsibility, visibility and ownership which simply translates to them having increased their problems, so they in turn want to make their problems your problems, want to make their stress yours.

The right to be mediocre (at work) is actually the right to pursue your own interests, to rest, to be with your family and to be free of the worries and stress of work. The problem is it can't just be asserted publicly—you can't let anybody else know you don't care about work and want to do the minimum because you never know which coworker has bought into all the myths and traps we have delineated in this chapter. Short of the general strikes of old, there's no collective action possible to assert this, so you are on your own.

In order to actually enjoy and assert this right you have to—paradoxically—approach mediocrity in an active and engaged manner; simply *being mediocre* is not enough to do job stacking. You need to become the King of Mediocrity.

Who is the King of Mediocrity?

A mediocre employee is not a bad employee at all, he is simply an employee that does the work that is requested of him in a satisfactory manner. He doesn't get into trouble, but then again he doesn't get into much of anything at all at work.

The King of Mediocrity is a mediocre employee that is completely self-aware of his mediocrity and embraces it. He realizes that work has lost all meaning, that all the talk about "loving" your work, or being "fulfilled" by your career, is just that: talk, marketing from big corporations so that they get more out of their employees' lives for the same amount of money—sometimes even for less—and to trick people into caring about doing menial tasks by making it seem they have a grander meaning. But instead of despairing, the King of Mediocrity simply takes advantage of the situation and is purposeful about his mediocre performance. He has no wish to climb any ladders, he simply does the bare minimum of satisfactory work without going beyond the call of duty and only gives the impression he will or has gone far beyond that line to personally get something out of it.

The King of Mediocrity is not concerned with improving productivity at the workplace, nor is he overly invested in giving more value to the business or making his team perform better. He maximizes his income and job security; he makes things better for himself and his family, not better for shareholders or managers. Therefore, he doesn't waste his idle time at work watching YouTube videos or browsing social media, because he'd rather spend that time on his own productive endeavors like having a second or third job, writing a book or perfecting his preferred craft or hobby.

In short, the King of Mediocrity is an employee who is aware of all the traps of modern employment and can therefore exploit employers instead of being exploited himself.

Now that you know what traps to avoid and what psychological outlook you should have regarding work, let's move on to how to actually stack jobs and how to manage them.

CHAPTER 6 BASICS OF JOB STACKING

The basics of job stacking consist of two main guiding principles, two things you need to be mentally prepared for, and three continuous actions you need to be doing.

The two main guiding principles

Job stacking is about security not riches

You need to understand that job stacking is mainly a defensive strategy, a way to hedge against the uncertainties and injustices of wage labor in the modern world. So you have to establish a basic level of income you need to live your life and then treat everything else you receive as extra money. **The idea of having multiple jobs is to create safety via redundancy, not to give you the life of a "rockstar millionaire."** For example, if you were doing fine with 5k a month but manage to land three jobs and are now making in total something like 15k a month, don't actually live a "15k-a-month life," at least until you have large enough savings to do so. Failing to do this and falling for the temptation to increase your consumption and standard of living is just increasing your risk exposure by living the same risky life but with more money. Remember, there is no true job security, so it's better to save your extra income or perhaps use it to make those investments you never got to get into because your paycheck ran out. Once I got the hang of job stacking, I was able to invest more than 5k a month and save 1k in cash every month while living a modest but comfortable life.

One job will be your main one

You need to understand that your jobs can never be equal or have the same value; you need to consciously assign one of the jobs priority status, whether because it's your favorite or because it's the one that pays you more—you choose the criteria but you will have to choose. This will be your main job, the one that breaks ties and sets your schedule, the one that if there is a risk of taking a hit to your reputation within a company you make sure it's not this one. If jobs are concubines or mistresses and you have a harem, then this is the "most favored" one. After that, you create the rest of the job hierarchy; some jobs you won't and shouldn't give a shit about, just treat whatever they pay you as a simple short-term bonus.

The two things you need to be mentally prepared for

Be comfortable coming up with and managing (succinct but genuine) excuses

You need to feel at ease excusing yourself to avoid conflicts between your jobs, without lying and without giving too many details. When we are nervous or feel guilty we tend to explain ourselves in too much detail. You need to mentally prepare to be in control of what you say. Avoid outright lying, but give as few details as possible. Practice saying short and true things like "Something else came up," "I won't be available," or "I have to take care of something." We will talk about handling scheduling conflicts in more detail in Chapter 10.

Be ready to get fired at any moment and be OK with it

It should not emotionally affect you to get fired. In the beginning, while you get used to it, having multiple jobs at the same time can be a bit like playing with fire, and there is a possibility that you will get burned until you get into the groove of things and find the right combination of jobs. If it deeply affects you getting a call or an email telling you "You're fired," you need to harden yourself. Keep in mind, **in the long term having multiple jobs is actually safer than having just one**. It'll be rare to lose two jobs at the same time or in short succession and, trust me, losing a job while having another one is often cause for laughter; I certainly laughed when I got fired from my second job ... the day I was starting my third.

The three continuous actions you need to be doing

Avoid creating patterns of behavior that damage trust

It is very important not to be repetitive with your excuses or evasive behavior in short periods of time, because once a pattern is established people will get progressively less tolerant and more suspicious of you. For instance, if you're always disconnecting from meetings people will start wondering why that is; or they'll wonder why you are never available when they write or call you, why you always sound distracted, or why you seem to always have issues at home. Rotate the excuses you use and the things that you say or do to avoid conflicts when juggling multiple jobs.

Avoiding increased responsibility and visibility

Remember, we no longer care about getting raises or climbing the ladder within some company, so do not increase your responsibility or visibility at all. Do not volunteer to do any tasks, do not try to impress your teammates or boss by tackling a complex issue, don't be the guy that is suggesting improvements to anything. Just stay quiet and do and say just enough to not get fired.

ABA: Always be Applying

The best time to be looking for work is when you're already employed, so always be applying to new jobs, that way whenever you need to make a substitution or add a new job to your stack you will have saved the time it takes to go through the whole application process, it also helps with receiving future offers since you will be on their system. Other benefits of ABA are that you have your finger constantly on the pulse of the job market and what it is currently demanding, you get a lot of real world practice with interviewing for jobs without the added stress of needing or being desperate for a job and lastly even if you don't get offers you have a ready made list of places you can apply o re apply to in the future as well as a wealth of connections with HR recruiters.

CHAPTER 7 JOB STACKING STRATEGIES

Perhaps having read thus far, you find yourself liking and understanding the idea behind job stacking but thinking there is no way you can pull it off; maybe your job is too complicated or too high-responsibility and you can't see yourself having two or more of them, or maybe your current job is not allowing employees to be remote. Don't worry; there is no one way to stack jobs. There are different strategies or approaches you can take to accommodate what you need or what you can comfortably handle. We'll see those strategies in this chapter.

There are many ways to approach job stacking depending on your current situation, your financial goals, and your time management skills. There is one particular strategy I advocate above the others and which is the main focus of this book; however, I feel the need to mention the others just to show that job stacking can be implemented in many ways and because the main strategy may not be appealing or useful to everybody. Here I divide these strategies according to some of the main parameters an employee might need to consider.

Strategies by job sustainability

Sustainable long-term job stacking

This approach consists in finding jobs that are a good match for job stacking so that you are able to keep all of them in the long run without hurting your reputation with any of your employers or at the very least in your designated main job. This strategy is the default assumption of this book—it's the one I had in mind when coming up with job stacking—and the advice contained within better fits this strategy, especially Chapter 8.

Unsustainable long term job stacking: rotating door

In this strategy ABA or "Always Be Applying" is an absolute necessity. The difference between this strategy and the long term approach is that you keep doing job stacking but the jobs you stack are constantly rotating, meaning you don't stay for long with them either because you keep quitting or keep getting fired. Under this strategy you're cycling through jobs so fast that going through different hiring processes sort of becomes your actual job. It's not sustainable because you will most likely be tarnishing your reputation with a lot of different employers and recruiters and it could come back to bite you later.

Short-term bursts

This strategy can be thought of as getting a special payment bonus. You stack another job for a short period of time, without tarnishing your reputation or burning yourself out. This strategy can also serve to get your feet wet or as a gateway to more long-term or complex job stacking approaches.

Strategies by amount of remote work

Full remote

All the jobs you stack are remote. This is the gold standard to strive for and a main assumption of this book.

Mixed remote

At least one of your jobs is not fully remote. Probable circumstances here are that you have one job, probably your main one, where despite the job itself being able to be done remotely, company policy restricts it in some sense. Job stacking is still possible under these circumstances, but it's a lot trickier. Any other job you stack under these conditions must be fully remote, otherwise job stacking becomes impossible. Appendix A is entirely dedicated to this tricky strategy.

No remote

Unless you can be in two places at one, this is a non-starter, job stacking requires at least one job to be fully remote.

Strategies by job seniority

Stacking jobs of equal seniority

This strategy is for people that feel comfortable in their current job and with their level of seniority and also find that they are in a good position to stack other equal or similar jobs.

Stacking mixed-seniority; the senior-as-a-junior approach

This strategy is for people that find that the jobs that tend to fit their current seniority are perhaps a bit too demanding or too high in visibility/responsibility to be able to stack more than one of them. Good news is you don't need to stack the same kind of jobs; you can stack different seniority positions. To implement this strategy you define your highest-responsibility job as your main one and then try to stack lower-responsibility or lower-seniority positions that won't be as demanding as your main job or, alternatively, you can completely forego any higher-seniority positions and simply stack all junior or low-responsibility jobs. To implement this strategy you will need to have a modified CV and LinkedIn profile. I talk about CV and LinkedIn management in Appendix B.

Strategies by financial maximization

Big bang

The central idea behind this strategy is to have one main job, but then get as many jobs as possible in a short period of time and try to collect at least one month of payment from all of them as you do almost no work at all. The main utility of this strategy is in getting you a lot of money quickly with very little hassle or concern about keeping any of the jobs, while not tarnishing your reputation at your designated main job. This is for people that simply want or need a large sum of money right now, perhaps to pay off some debts or get the down payment on a home.

A consulting company of one

Under this strategy you take many jobs, more than you could reasonably handle on your own, but instead of working them yourself *or* doing nothing at all, you contract the jobs out to other people and keep a cut of the salary. Your main job then becomes managing communications with your "employers" and managing your subcontractors.

Don't feel that you have to stick with a single approach forever; you can always alternate between them to see what feels more comfortable or what aligns better with your needs and situation. Alternatively, you could implement multiple strategies at the same time but apply them to different groups of companies. For instance, you could be more protective or conservative with jobs you feel you can stack more sustainably in the long term, while at the same time trying to collect one month of salary from a multitude of companies you really don't care about, thus creating a mix between the long-term sustainable and big bang strategies.

Whichever strategy or combination thereof you decide to implement, the advice in the following chapters will help you to do so carefully and successfully.

CHAPTER 8 CHOOSING THE RIGHT JOBS TO STACK

In order to be able to stack jobs, you must work in a certain kind of environment. The contents of this book simply don't and can't apply to all possible jobs, workplaces and companies.

What kind of jobs should be stacked?

The only hard restriction is that the jobs have to be fully remote. If the job can't be done remotely then there is no chance to stack it. Other than that, for most people reading this book, getting another job similar to the one they already have is what will work for job stacking. This is one of the basic premises we're working from: you already have your CV ready, you already know how to do your job—simply get another one.

However, if for whatever reason you're deciding to diversify or "start fresh," then the best jobs to get are the ones where you spend most of the time doing nothing as you wait for work to be assigned to you. Under the careerist paradigm, a job where you do nothing is supposed to be terrible for you and your career, as you don't develop skills or relevant experience. But for a job stacker, a job where you do very little is basically free money: At least in theory, the best situation would be stacking as many jobs as you can where you do as little as possible.

Jobs where you have some autonomy to finish your tasks, and can be left alone most of the time, are preferred as you have a lot more power in deciding how to administer your time between jobs.

Jobs where you get paid commission, or where your income depends on "performance" or how many tasks you close, tend not to be as good for job stacking, as either you will be pressured to meet quotas, or your pay won't be as good. Remember that job stacking is about abusing the fact that, in most jobs, you don't get back what you put in, and thus you're paid the same whether you give them 10% or 100% effort. A job that *does* give you back what you put in goes against that principle and so is not a strong candidate for job stacking.

Choosing the right position; you can(not) become a manager

Not all positions or jobs work for job stacking; if your work inherently requires you to be in constant meetings where you are an active participant (what I call "Active Meetings") or can't be done remotely at all, then unfortunately job stacking might not be possible.

The other types of work that are not conducive to job stacking are high-responsibility or high-visibility positions, such as that of a manager. The reason should be obvious: the more responsibility you have, the higher the expectations are about your performance, which means you will need to be more engaged in that particular job.

Increasing your visibility and level of responsibility is the traditional way of earning more money, the way to "climb the ladder." I hope it's clear by now that climbing the ladder is not worth it in our current times, so you need to avoid as much exposure to direct responsibility as possible—you do not want to be in any kind of "leadership" position. For instance, you can be a senior software developer as long as you're not the technical lead, or as long as you are not the only senior on the project. You want to be a soldier in the trenches, being handed more or less simple tasks to complete; you don't want to be the guy "making decisions" or going to meetings all day.

There is only one exception to this and that's when you do what I call an "initiative drive," which simply put is a proactive attempt on your part to increase the company's (or your team's) trust in you, so that later you can be better left to your own devices (see Appendix C for more).

Don't confuse the above for being a hermit, though; you are avoiding responsibility and visibility to higher-ups, not avoiding interaction with your coworkers in general. If you're not the social type, don't worry; this isn't about being "social" either, it's about simple communication—letting people know you're available when they ask.

Now we need to talk about how to recognize the kind of environment that is conducive to job stacking.

Choosing the right company

The keywords for choosing the right company to work for are: "expectations"—what does the company expect from its employees?; and "trust"—does the company trust its employees?

Keeping this in mind I catalogue companies in three ways: Bad Companies, Mediocre Companies and Good Companies.

Don't let the names deceive you though; you don't actually want to work for a "good" company nor do you want to avoid a mediocre one. Just the opposite: we actually want to aim for mediocre companies. But what are the differences? How can you tell one from the others? Let's define our terms.

Bad companies

Bad companies, simply put, are companies where trust in employees is low. They come in two flavors: high expectations (the "traditional" kind of bad company; definitely avoid these) and low expectations (these are harder to find but slightly less bad).

Low trust, high expectations

These are companies that don't trust their employees but still have high expectations of them. Bad companies usually handle projects and clients that are terrible and demand "proof" that "work is being done"; bad companies also tend to be "client-centric" instead of "team-centric" or "employee-centric," which means they throw employees under the bus instead of "training" their clients into more appropriate processes. You will find they often demand you install tracking devices even on your personal computer. Their processes are totally immature and they tend to have a "bottom line" mentality.

Bad companies should be avoided, but they can sometimes be worthwhile for short periods of time if no other opportunities arise. They should *never* be your primary job, nor should you try to stack multiple bad jobs together—that's an almost certain way to get burned out and/or fired and be out of jobs fast. Bad companies not only expect you to "deliver," they also expect a lot of free and unaccounted hours from you. If something breaks, time spent fixing it can't be billed to their precious clients, so you are expected to be working for free a lot of the time. They will also tend not to value any input or suggestions you may give, which, as we will see later in the book, takes away a valuable chance to make it seem like you are performing admirably and are invested in the company. Keep in mind that despite all their tracking, because their processes are immature, it actually takes time for them to catch "slackers" (people not performing to whatever standard they have), which is what in the end causes the lack of trust and "high expectations," but it's a perfect space for you to cash in on a few months of pay without doing much—just expect to eventually be fired when they do catch you.

I once got a second job at a bad company and didn't do much for months even when my computer was being tracked and screenshots were being taken every five minutes—their processes were that atrocious. What's even funnier is that I had made it through their "test period" and even gotten an above average review. I was now "in" the company, they were really happy with me, and they were even going to pay for an online course of my choosing, until a couple of days later, on a Friday, the software project I was working on stopped running on my personal computer and I had no idea why. I was told time spent solving that issue could not be billed, so I didn't work on it at all that day, much less over the weekend.

When our Monday daily meeting came up, I reported that I still had the issue reported on Friday and hadn't been able to work on any assigned tasks. Five minutes after the end of the meeting and not even a week after having been told my performance had been good and the company was happy with me...I received a phone call and was told I was fired. No warnings, no chance to explain anything, no second chances—just fired. Why? Because I didn't work for free over the weekend to solve the issue I was having. This is what low trust, high expectations looks like.

Low trust, low expectations

In this case the company doesn't trust its employees, but neither does it demand or expect much from them. It's rare to see a bad company like this, but they are out there. The advantage this type of bad company has over the other is that the lowered expectations reduce stress and allow you to get away with doing less. If you find a company like this, it could be worth it to try to job stack with. The general warnings for the first type of bad company apply here as well, but also be aware that at any point the company could decide to start increasing what it expects from its employees. One could argue that this type of company doesn't really exist in a stable state but is just a weird transitional stage to the more "traditional" bad company, so don't get too comfortable.

Good companies: high trust, high expectations

Good companies *do* trust their employees, but given the highly competitive nature of the work they perform and/or the prestige of the company, they also tend to have very high expectations from their employees and tend to have a greater pool of talented applicants to pick and choose from. You will find you have a lot of "freedom" in these companies (you won't really be tracked like in bad companies), and there will be lots of cool perks and benefits, but at the end of the day your job will be highly complex and highly demanding. You might end up eventually finding your performance under more scrutiny than in a bad company, simply because you won't be able to hide within the gaps of their bad internal processes; they may not track you or be on your case the way a bad company will, but they have highly developed metrics for how each employee should be performing in their given role. Another risk is that you simply may not measure up to the skill level they actually need; maybe you made it through the interview but can't really perform on the job. It happens. You may even find that you last longer underperforming in a bad company than in a good one.

We tend to want to avoid good companies because they are unnecessarily stressful and competitive. However, if you find you have the skill and the discipline to handle a good company's workload with consistency, then go for it. Use your judgment and see if you can maybe stack another, less demanding job on top—but don't ever stack two jobs that are both at good companies.

I've worked at good companies on two separate occasions and lasted about a month each time. I shined in the interviews but then found out after induction that I simply couldn't keep up with what they were doing. I just didn't measure up to their expectations, so they let me go, albeit in a more dignified and serious manner than at the bad company I worked for, but there were still no warnings, explanations or second chances. Remember that with these companies there is a weird competitive climate that the high expectations and prestigious "pedigree" of the company create, which just translates into a lot of unnecessary stress that could result in burnout.

Mediocre companies: high trust, low expectations

Mediocre companies are the perfect mix of trust and expectations, and as such they are our main target for holding multiple jobs. They trust their employees but don't expect too much of them because they don't have the prestige, high complexity, and/or demanding projects that good companies get. Mediocre companies are aspirational and want to imitate the good ones' "culture" and how they treat their employees, so you will often get all or most of the perks of working at "good" companies without the stress or burden of the highly demanding and highly complex projects they work on. Mediocre companies will also tend to be less "client-centric," since they tend to have a diverse enough portfolio of clients, and so they tend to be more protective of their employees; they don't always bend over backwards for their customers or clients, which gives you, the employee, a bigger buffer not to be a "high performer." Mediocre companies will make it much easier for you to be the King of Mediocrity.

I have never been fired or let go from a mediocre company, in fact quite the opposite: they have fought to keep me whenever I've been about to change jobs. It's thanks to my work at mediocre companies, and how well I've done in them in comparison with good or bad ones, that I came up with the tactics, techniques and very idea of this book. I realized I could easily work two or more jobs since I was able to be a valued employee without having to exert myself too strongly or give them my full potential.

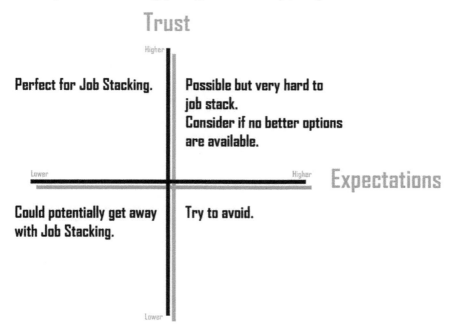

CHAPTER 9: OFFICE SETUP
AND TOOLS FOR JOB STACKING

This and the following chapter are probably the most important of the guide. They handle what is most likely the biggest source of doubt about engaging in job stacking: How do you handle conflicting meetings or unexpected calls and avoid being found out? Let's begin addressing these issues by starting with the hardware and office setup you'll need in order to stack jobs safely.

Multiple computers

Job stacking is easier with multiple computers. I don't recommend doing it with only one, or having information or software from more than one job on a single computer; ideally we want one computer per job stacked. The reason is simple: we want to avoid any potential situation in which mixing unrelated job information is possible. Each work computer should only have its appropriate work-related information and programs on it, especially if any type of employee activity or network traffic is being tracked.

Imagine that you are on a call in which you are required to share your screen. Suddenly notifications from your other job start popping in, or your calendar alerts you on-screen of a meeting from a different job. Needless to say, this would be disastrous. We want to avoid any potential situation like that.

It is essential that each job you have live in its own computer world, easily accessible by you. True, if there is no actual tracking being done, someone who is extremely detail-oriented and disciplined could probably manage to close all unrelated work information and programs and also avoid notifications, or perhaps deftly rotate between virtual desktops, but it is too much of a risk for most of us, and there is a lot of opacity regarding tracking—sometimes you can't be 100% sure your employer is not tracking *something*. So it's better to avoid these problems altogether and simply encapsulate and isolate each job in its own world, its own computer. That way there is a virtually 0% chance of something from one job spilling into another by mistake.

Handling multiple computers

Some people have enough office and desk space to have several computers open at the same time; many even enjoy that type of setup already. Gamers, for instance, tend to already have more than one computer, one for work and the other for gaming, so if you're one of those people who are already used to handling multiple computers or displays and see no problem with simply having them all open at the same time, then jump to the next chapter; however, if you're not sure how you would handle having multiple computers, feel you don't have the space, or simply do not want to be switching between monitors or keyboards all the time, this section explains how to tie multiple computers together into a single monitor and a single keyboard and mouse—saving lots of space while we are at it.

KVM Switches

The trick here is to get something called a "KVM Switch," KVM standing for "Keyboard, Video and Mouse." A KVM switch is a piece of hardware that lets you connect multiple computers to a single mouse, a single keyboard and a single video output signal and then switch between computers as if you were changing TV channels. Each time you switch, all keyboard, mouse and video functions are channeled to the active computer. This way we not only save desk or office space, we save ourselves from the hassle of multiple or additional keyboards, mouses or monitors. The basic premise of what a KVM switch does looks something like this:

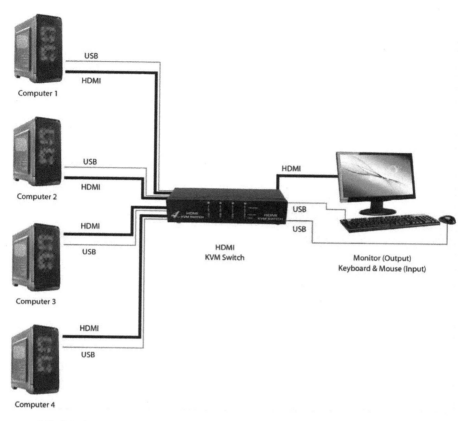

Multiple computers, one point of control and interaction.
Image taken from https://www.hdcabling.co.za

KVM switches are not some super fancy complicated piece of technology; you can buy them online for around $150 and they come with easy-to-read setup instructions—speaking of which, setting them up is very easy, especially today with basically all cables being either HDMI or USB. All you do is connect all your computers, plus your mouse and keyboard, to the switch's panel, then connect the output cable to a monitor (or multiple monitors if your KVM switch allows it), and you're done—to change control between computers, all you do is press a button.

As an example of how much space one can save with this kind of setup, let me show you this candid picture of my own original home office space. The following picture is what my very humble and very small desk looked like when I started getting serious about having multiple jobs. When the picture was taken I only had two, so notice there are two (closed) laptops but one monitor and one keyboard and mouse set. Please also notice the lovely drawing my 6-year-old boy left on my desk.

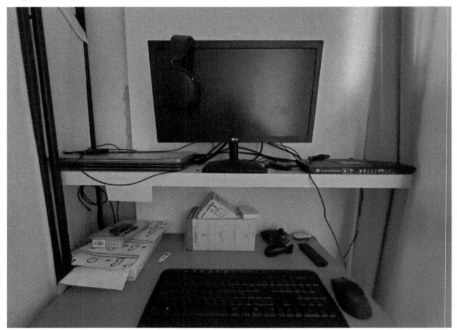

The KVM Switch is the flat thing with the little blue lights

Keep in mind that while you are indeed "switching" between computers, the computers themselves don't get interrupted or shut down when the switch happens and anything that is directly attached to them and not the KVM switch itself—any cameras, microphones, hard drives or USB devices—do not "switch" control, and keep running as if nothing had changed. So we need to be extra careful when handling microphones, headphones/speakers or cameras.

Microphones, headphones and cameras

Since we are now handling multiple computers, having one or multiple wired headset or microphones becomes very cumbersome, so it's best to job stack with a wireless headset with its own microphone. The wireless headset and microphone will make it easier to switch between computers or meetings on the fly without having to connect or disconnect physical devices, which is essential to managing conflicting calls or meetings as we shall see in chapter 10.

If you decide to go the KVM route, there are some things you need to keep in mind. If you connect your camera or headset to the KVM switch, then whenever you switch computers, you will be switching those devices as well, this means if you're in a boring meeting from one job that still requires a camera but you decide to work on something from your other job, on your other computer, and you "switch" to it, then your camera will be disconnected from the meeting since it will now "belong" to the new computer. Remember, with KVM switches your computers are still isolated from each other, we simply change control between them. Same will happen to your microphone headphones or speakers. Anything connected to the KVM switch will only work on the *currently selected computer* you're using. So we kind of want to keep any audio or camera footage outside the control of our dandy little switch, just to avoid any issues.

The recommendations here are simple: if you are regularly required to have the camera on during meetings, then connect the camera to the computer itself, not the KVM switch. With the headphones and mic the same logic applies and my recommendation is to use a Bluetooth headset, since it is fully wireless (no need to plug anything into any PC or switch) and you can match it up with any computer in just a few clicks. A Bluetooth headset will allow you to switch computers without the audio switching too, and if you ever do need to switch audio, it's only a few clicks from your keyboard and you're done.

A possible exception to using KVM switches

There is one particular case where using a KVM switch might not be the best arrangement: if one or more of your jobs uses some kind of tracking software. I talk more in depth about how to manage tracking software in Appendix D, but the main idea is that you want to have some recorded activity on your computer every so often and if you have a KVM switch it can make it slightly more annoying having to constantly switch back and forth than if you simply had all your computers open and available at the same time and all you did was move your mouse. It's up to you to decide what works best in your situation.

With our workstation ready, we are now good to move on to take advantage of it to handle those dreaded conflicting meetings you may still think make job stacking impossible or a hassle.

CHAPTER 10 MANAGING CONFLICTS:
MEETINGS AND CALLS

Meetings are a prevalent part of the types of jobs that are compatible with job stacking, and they're a big mental hurdle for people considering holding multiple concurrent jobs. People fear the idea of having meetings from different jobs come up at the same time. "What about meetings?" was almost always one of the first questions I was asked when discussing the idea of multiple jobs with friends and family. Fear not: In this chapter I will show you not only that the probability of having conflicting meetings is incredibly low, but also how to handle them if such a thing does happen. Let's start discussing the nature of meetings first.

Types of meetings

We can define meetings as coming in three basic types: meetings where you need to pay attention and participate most of the time; meetings where you need to pay attention only at a specific time; and meetings where you do not need to pay attention. We'll call them active meetings, semi-active meetings, and passive meetings, respectively.

Active meetings

Let's address active meetings first since they are the most concerning. An active meeting is one where you have to actively participate, meaning you have to provide coherent feedback or perhaps even lead the meeting; they also tend to be ones where you can't hide your disinterest or disengagement because the number of participants is not very high and you can't hide in the folds of their conversation. One-on-one meetings with superiors are the perfect example, but there are also "surprise" meetings where a coworker suddenly wants to get a hold of you to go over something.

It will be basically impossible to stack jobs if your line of work requires your day to be filled to the brim with active meetings. Notice I say line of work and not "current job" because if the high volume of meetings is just how your employer does things but is not inherent to what you do, job stacking will still be possible if your other employers are more laid back regarding active meetings.

Most jobs don't require people to be in active meetings all day, however, so let me show you why you shouldn't be afraid and shouldn't let the prospect of meetings stop you, using simple math.

Let's say you have a job where active meetings could happen at any time without warning during a regular 8-hour workday. Then let's say we divide those 8 hours into 30-minute periods or time slots in which a meeting could happen without your control. We will get 16 possible time slots for meetings to occur and each time slot would represent 1/16 of your day. Now let's say you get another job and we do the same breakup of the 8 hours. What is the probability of both jobs scheduling a meeting in the same 30 minute time slot? The math is simple: 1/16 x 1/16 = 1/256 or roughly 0.004%. That's how low the chances are of having two active meetings overlap during your day.

On top of the already low chances of getting overlapping meetings or calls, there is a very concrete measure you can implement to reduce the risk of conflicting meetings even further: get jobs in different time zones. If the jobs you get start and end at different times, you'll reduce the probability of getting some common meetings like "morning all-hands" or "daily standups" happening at the same time.

So again, don't let the fear of overlapping meetings keep you from getting multiple jobs—the math is in your favor.

Handling overlapping active meetings

We can't just assume it will never happen, though, and remember that feeling comfortable with making excuses without lying is one of the main things we need to mentally prepare for in order to pursue job stacking, so let's see how we can prepare and handle the issue. There are two lines of defense against overlapping or conflicting active meetings. Let's see:

The first line of defense is rescheduling. Attempting to reschedule should be your first resort: If the meeting is impromptu and you have any say in the matter of whether the meeting happens or not, just reschedule. A very easy, effective and noncommittal excuse is to say you need a couple of minutes to handle something at home and you'll join soon (don't specify what it is you need to take care of, *ever*), then simply say the issue you thought was going to take a couple of minutes will actually take longer and you need to reschedule.

The second line of defense is to have technical issues. Let's say your attempts at a friendly reschedule have failed, or you have rescheduled too much and are trying to avoid creating a pattern (remember that doing the same thing or using the same excuse over and over creates a pattern and thus grounds for suspicion). Just join the meeting and immediately create technical problems: disconnect your headphones so you can't hear anybody, disconnect your microphone so people can't hear you, or activate airplane mode on your computer so you lose your internet connection. Then you can excuse yourself and say you're having technical problems. You can do this to pop in and out of meetings for long periods of time and no one will think anything of it; everyone has technical problems some of the time.

Now let's say both your lines of defense have failed. So you're trapped, as you can't reschedule or it is risky to have technical problems because you have used those excuses too much; they've already brought it to your attention and they are not very accommodating anymore; you gotta do the meeting and do it now. What do you do? This is where the second principle of job stacking comes into play: You will unfortunately need to choose which of the jobs you have is the main one and satisfy it while letting down the others.

Semi-active and passive meetings

The quintessential semi-active meeting is the "daily standup" where everyone takes turns to give a status update on what they were working on the previous day, your participation is required but only for a fraction of the meeting, only passing attention is needed, since after you give your update odds are you won't have to participate anymore. Passive meetings are your typical (and dreaded) team-wide or "all hands'" meetings, they are usually about useless company or team stuff that nobody really cares about. While everyone else rightly hates these meetings, they are the best types of meetings for job stacking and the favorite of the king of mediocrity; the more people are involved in them, the less you have to pay attention, the better for you. Remember, don't ever feel bad about not paying attention, you don't have to do it yourself because there is always somebody else that is and can give you any relevant info later, plus if nobody pays attention then you can't be singled out for not doing it either, it's a win-win, passive meetings are basically free money.

Handling overlapping semi-active and passive meetings

Semi-active and passive meetings are a breeze to handle if you followed my previous advice of getting a Bluetooth headset and a different computer or device for each job you have. The first two lines of defense against active meetings also work for semi-active ones, and the difference is that the game isn't over if you can't avoid them happening. Let's see what else we can do.

Prior preparations

There are some previous hardware preparations you need to do before we even get to the moment of the meeting. The very first thing you need to do is mute or disconnect the default microphone from all your computers. I don't mean "mute yourself" in the context of the meeting, I mean you need to completely disable the default microphone on all your computers. You don't want that microphone to be working at any point or you run the risk of accidentally having the people in one job hear you talking about things from a different job. Once the default microphones are completely disabled, take your Bluetooth headset and pair it with all your computers, for easy connection (and disconnection) in the future; you will of course have to pair it with one computer at a time. Remember that with Bluetooth it's one thing to have your computer know about the device (pairing) and another to actually connect to it (using the headset), so what we are doing now is letting the computer know about the headset so that we can connect it later. Finally, have the default speakers on all your devices be muted by default—this time mute is fine, no need to disable them; this is to avoid the risk of having the sound from one meeting spill over into a different one.

Practice connecting and disconnecting the Bluetooth headset, from one computer to the next, so you feel comfortable doing it. A good idea is to have a practice meeting with a friend and verify that when you disconnect the Bluetooth headset, your computers' microphones stay disabled and that audio doesn't leak out from their speakers. Once that's confirmed, you're ready for multiple meetings.

Once the meetings begin

Sign in to one meeting first and pay attention to what's happening; assess if your participation will be required soon, later, or never. If your participation is not required soon, stay in the meeting but disconnect your headset and then join the other meetings once again assessing when is your participation most likely to be if at all.

Remember that all these meetings are mostly bullshit and a huge waste of time; all we're doing is keeping tabs on whether you need to say something or not, basically if someone addresses you directly.

To keep tabs on the meeting you need to be switching your headphones back and forth at regular intervals to hear how the meetings are progressing but also have the chat log of the different meeting clients open and visible at all times to see if for whatever reason they are trying to contact you there. Remember that if you don't respond right away the first thing people think is you're having technical issues, so they might try to contact you by chat. Take advantage of all the little visible cues modern meeting clients like Hangouts or MS Teams offer, like the little "sound waves" that they show when someone is talking; if all of a sudden all of them stop for several seconds, that's a red flag that it might be your turn to talk.

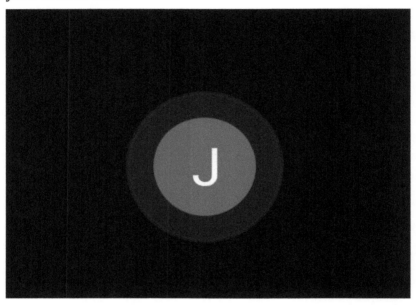

An example of a visual cue that someone is currently speaking (from Google Hangouts in this case). Notice the little shade or wave around the circled letter.

Participating in meetings

The trick is simply not to actively participate; you want to be invisible most of the time. Don't tell little jokes or ask questions or try to feign interest; you can do all of this when the meetings are *not* overlapping and in that case you're free to devote more attention, but if the meetings are overlapping your attention should be on keeping tabs on all your meetings to see what is happening. Remember, you can also apply the two defenses described for active meetings, having to take care of something or having technical issues, at any point during one of these meetings to avoid having to participate. However, if at some point you must participate, don't worry or be nervous; realize that while you yourself know you have multiple jobs, the others don't, so anything "odd" they might notice about your behavior like responding late, shallow responses, or asking to have something repeated, won't alert them to the fact that you have another job or are in another meeting. They will simply think you're at best having technical problems or at worst not paying much attention. It'll be fine—remember, we are job stacking, we don't care about getting "promoted" in a particular workplace. Simply not getting fired is what we want, and no one will fire you for not being super sharp and attentive in some (or even most) meetings. In any case, you can always make up for being "distracted" by paying more attention and being more active in other meetings when there is no overlap. The point is to throw people off by not creating patterns.

What about meetings where the camera has to be on?

Turning on your camera for meetings can be a bit of a problem, but fortunately it's a problem we can handle. Let's see how.

Adjusting your cameras

You need to position your computers or webcams in such a way that none of them should ever capture your hands or forearms; that way no one can see what you're doing with them. Your cameras should also never show your other computers or monitors (if you have them), otherwise you risk showing your work from another company, or even worse, a different meeting in progress. Imagine having two overlapping meetings and the faces of your colleagues from one job show up in the meeting of one of your other jobs through your camera—not good. So ensure that never happens by correctly positioning your camera. Don't worry if to get the positioning done correctly you have to block part of what the camera captures; no one will really mind as they can't do anything about how much space you have in your home office or the layout of it.

Managing yourself in front of the camera

Having the cameras correctly positioned fixes 99% of any potential problems you may encounter, as your hands should be out of sight and your other work invisible, but there is one more issue you need to pay attention to: If you need to talk in one meeting but not the other, it will show on the camera that you are talking, which looks weird. However, mitigating this problem is as easy as turning the camera off for a little bit in whatever meeting(s) you're not supposed to be talking in and then turning it back on; no one will think anything of it as long as you comply with having the camera on most of the time. People are only likely to take issue when someone *never* follows the rules and/or complains about them, so remember never to express discontent about having to turn your camera on, much less argue about it, because then any time you do take the camera off it will be seen as you not cooperating. Alternatively, a good mixup to avoid turning off the camera without notice all the time is to simply pretend you're talking to someone else in your home office not visible to the camera by moving your head to the side or making little hand gestures (like "wait") to someone next to you; you can do this and *then* turn your camera off, and people will simply think you're handling something at home that shouldn't be shown on camera. It's fun.

A special note about meetings when you begin a new job

When you're starting a new job you will have plenty of meetings to introduce you to processes, tools, projects, etc. It is easier to manage starting a new job if you get time off from your current job during the first few days of starting the new one. This makes handling all the new information, calls and meetings a lot easier since you only need to worry about one job for the first few days. However, all of these initial meetings are useless and a waste of time; they're formalities, and while you will have to be present in the meetings, you can probably safely not pay attention to them and focus on tasks from your other jobs. So it's probably also okay if you decide not to take time off your current job. If, during a meeting, they ask you if you have any questions, you will want to avoid responding with a dry "no," because not having questions can be interpreted as you not paying attention. A more charming alternative is to say something like "I don't have any questions now, but I'm sure I will soon"; this response is not a lie and also shows you have a good attitude and are invested in the future of your new job. It shows you are indeed new and don't fully grasp all of what they're saying, but that you are committed to learning it in the future. As for the contents of the meeting, don't worry; you are new, and humans don't learn by exposition dumps, but by slowly getting acquainted with something and with practice, so you will get plenty of opportunities to be taught what you need to do and what you need to know. No one is expecting you to come out of those meetings knowing anything, which is the main reason why they are a huge waste of everyone's time.

CHAPTER 11 A Day in the Life of a Job Stacker

This chapter is a simple walkthrough of a somewhat more stressful day than usual (due to overlapping calls). The idea is just to convey a concrete image of what it looks like to stack jobs when a conflict of calls happens. It is of course an amalgamation of things that I've experienced and not a chronicle of any one particular day.

Let's say I'm stacking two jobs as a senior software developer; we'll call them Job 1 and Job 2. Job 1 is on Central Time and Job 2 on Pacific Time. Working from home, I'm on Central Time.

I start Job 1 at 9am, just checking email and dropping good-mornings in the chat so that people know I'm at my computer. We have a daily standup meeting at 9:30am, so I connect my wireless headset to the Job 1 computer and then connect to the meeting. I give my update explaining that I've finished a task, and I get assigned a new one that is due in a couple of days. After the daily I immediately switch to my other computer and start working on small tasks for Job 2, so that I'll have a more complete update for *their* daily standup, which is happening at 11 my time, 9am Pacific time.

Before starting the meeting for Job 2 I disconnect the wireless headset from Job 1's computer and connect now to Job 2's computer. The daily standup meeting for Job 2 starts. I give my update explaining that I've advanced pretty far in my task, but it isn't done yet, and it's going to take me a bit longer to complete. I say this to buy myself more time, just in case. As soon as I give my update, I leave the wireless headset connected to Job 2's computer, but switch to Job 1 and start working on some small tasks while I listen to Job 2's meeting.

After the meeting, I check my calendar and see I have no more meetings from either job until around 5 hours from now, when I have a Job 2 meeting. So I simply decide which task from which job has more priority. I decide to work on Job 2 since I just completed a task for Job 1 and the newly assigned task from them is not due soon.

I keep working at my own pace for around 4 hours, checking communications on both jobs just in case someone is trying to reach me or tell me something. At one point someone from Job 1 wants to go over something with me, so I switch computers, connect my wireless headset to Job 1's computer and jump in. I share my screen without fear because there is nothing related to Job 2 on this computer. While I'm sharing the screen I do a quick switch to Job 2's computer to make sure no one is requiring my attention there. This little Job 1 call helping my coworker takes me around thirty minutes. My next meeting is in half an hour so I decide to take a break and don't work on anything until the meeting.

Job 2 meeting starts and it's a team-wide meeting about some new process and tool. After a few minutes, I switch to Job 1's computer and see that my team lead wants to talk and is currently calling me. I write to him and tell him to give me a few minutes. I disconnect my headset from Job 2 (without disconnecting from the meeting or turning off the camera) and connect to Job 1. The call with my Job 1 team lead starts; he has some questions about something new I implemented. Before starting to go over stuff I ask him to give me a minute. I mute my mic for Job 1, switch to Job 2, and without connecting my headset, use my computer's speakers to hear what they're talking about briefly; it seems they're not talking about anything that would relate to me. I disconnect the camera and mute Job 2's speakers. I then unmute my mic in Job 1 as I switch to that computer and start to go over whatever my team lead wanted to talk about. I keep switching to Job 2 here and there, quickly, just to see if people are still talking or trying to contact me via chat; so far, nothing. Switch back to Job 1's computer (remember, my headset has been on Job 1 the whole time) and keep working on the issue with my team lead and now another more junior developer, who is handling a related task, joins the call. Eventually I don't need to share my screen anymore, as it's the junior's turn now. I immediately switch to Job 2 and it turns out people are asking me something and I haven't responded yet. I bring up the text chat inside the call and write to them that I'm having issues with connectivity. I set Job 2's computer to airplane mode to lose all connectivity, disconnecting myself from both the call and any chat clients that would make me appear as "available." Switch to Job 1 for a bit and engage in the meeting. I then ask for a break and to reschedule it for later because something else has come up and I need to take care of it. We reschedule for tomorrow, I thank them, disconnect my headset from Job 1, switch to Job 2, reconnect everything network-wise and jump back into the Job 2 meeting. The meeting is almost ending, but they see me reconnect and, acting all happy that I'm back, ask me my opinion on implementing the new tool. I tell them something non-committal, like that it's too early and we'll see what happens. The meeting ends and I take a sigh of relief. I decide to take my lunch now that all scheduled meetings seem to be over; if anyone wants anything, I'll just tell them I'm out eating and will get back to them later.

Nothing eventful happens. 5pm Central comes and Job 1 is over; no one from there will bother me now. I'm supposed to stay until 5pm Pacific or 7pm Central for Job 2, but no way I'm doing that. I stay until 6pm Central working on my newest Job 1 task; I make sure to work enough to have something to say, a basic update on my work for next morning's meeting. Another day handling more than one job concludes.

CONCLUSION

The first time I tried having more than one job, it was before the COVID-19 pandemic and widespread remote work. I had some work-from-home days at the place where I worked, so I figured I could pull off having a second, fully remote job if I played my cards right. I couldn't handle it for more than a few weeks—I made too many mistakes and wasn't prepared for what it would entail on the logistics side. Despite failing, the experience left me open to the idea that having more than one full-time job was possible. Years later, this time having a fully remote job, I decided to try it again. I created a plan to handle both jobs, started interviewing, got another job and took it without telling anybody about it. I thought at the time that it was going to be a short-term affair, a one- or two-months' bonus to my salary—no way I could last having two jobs. But to my surprise, I was able to keep it going for longer than I ever thought I would last. I was managing it just fine. I eventually added a third job; again, same idea as the first time—I thought it would be a one- or two-month thing—but yet again I lasted longer than I expected. Eventually I kept pushing until I hit my limit: The amount of jobs and meetings and stress was too much to handle; despite the money being very good, I felt it wasn't worth it. So I started dialing it back, first abruptly, later more slowly until I felt comfortable and happy again with the amount of jobs I was handling.

The new COVID era has accelerated the arrival of fully remote jobs, and it's a good opportunity to try stacking them. You don't have to jump in fully committed from the get-go—take your time, try it out, leave it, come back a few months or years later and then try again. But I do encourage you to try it for yourself at least once; otherwise you'll never see how comfortable you might be with job stacking or how much you can get away with. And if the COVID reforms are not meant to last and everyone goes back to the office, then at least take the chance now and get some more money while you can.

I hope you've enjoyed reading my little book and that it is useful to you even if you're not planning on committing to job stacking soon or for very long.

Thanks for reading.

APPENDIXES

Appendix A Managing partially remote jobs

If you're reading this, you're interested in pursuing job stacking, but your current job is not fully remote and you don't want to leave it to find another one that is. This is something that is very hard but technically possible to do.

You need to be constantly assessing if it's worth continuing or if you should reconsider job stacking and leave it for another time when it becomes easier to do. You need to pay special attention to how much of your live attention your second job requires of you— if it's full of mandatory meetings and little calls, then things will probably not work out.

Your second job obviously has to be *fully* remote; if it's not, then job stacking is impossible. A lot of things depend on the kind of job you're getting; ideally it should be a laid-back job from a mediocre company that gives you a lot of freedom.

The game plan is to protect your privacy at your non-remote work while you handle communications with the second. To do this you need to minimize consuming any resources of your office in service of your second job. Using office resources increases the possibility of you getting found out and fired. For instance, if you have a meeting to attend at your second job, don't use a meeting room from your office; instead excuse yourself for a bit and take it outside, or at worst go to the bathroom at your office. This also means you will probably need to have a good phone with copious amounts of data in order to take calls and be in meetings as well as handle chat clients. In this scenario, your phone serves as the "other computer" you should have for job stacking; your phone is the device that encapsulates your other job. So be sure to have a decent phone.

Deciding to actually do work from your second job at your office, instead of simply handling communications, will depend on how restrictive your company is and how much privacy you have where you work. The safer way to do work for your remote job from the offices of your non-remote one is to leave a computer at home, on and online all day, so you can connect remotely into it from your office using specialized remote access and control software. Again, remember to always assess what's worth trying to get away with; if your current non-remote or partially remote job is very low-trust, job stacking can get very hard to do. Companies always monitor network traffic in the office, but many times it is simply for audit and security purposes; they're looking for specific security red flags, not necessarily looking at everything everyone does, so if you have enough privacy at your workstation it might even be safe to open your second job's documents or tasks since they are "work"-related and therefore don't raise red flags, though there are so many hidden risks I can't fully endorse it. Instead try to do everything from your phone if possible.

One last important thing to remember is that whenever one begins a new job, the first few weeks are always full of meetings, tutorials and introductions, so when you're about to start your new job, make sure you stay home from your current one for a couple of days; ask for some days off or special work-from-home time, but be sure you're not at your office for at least the first three days of your (new) second job.

Appendix B Managing modified LinkedIn Profiles and CVs

If you're reading this you're probably interested in pursuing the mixed-seniority job stacking strategy, or in other words: stacking jobs that are actually below your seniority.

If you have a high seniority level and are concerned about not being able to handle the workload of two or more jobs of your same seniority, you can always just get a more junior-level position. For this all you have to do is modify your CV to reduce your experience. You should also create an alternate LinkedIn profile that reflects this CV.

Keep in mind, we are not inventing "fake CVs" whole-cloth; on the contrary, the information will be real. Your name can't be fake, of course, and as far as your experience is concerned, we are not making things up, but rather adapting your stated experience to fit roles that require less experience than you really have. Any "fakeness" that arises will come from having to do things like changing dates and little else. Simply create a CV you're comfortable with that fits the positions you are aiming for, but I highly recommend you leave your current or last employer as your current or last employer (even if the roles are not the same), because it makes it easier to avoid mistakes or any unnatural lack of recollections of your most recent experience if asked about it. It would be weird if you couldn't remember your current employer in an interview because you didn't remember which one you put on your CV, right? There's also another reason for doing this, which is that LinkedIn actually hides your profile from recruiters working for your current employer, which will also avoid some potential weirdness. After you're done creating your alternate CV, then move on to creating your alternate LinkedIn profile.

To create the alternate profile I recommend playing with your real name. For instance if your name is Dwight Kurt Schneider you could have two LinkedIn profiles, one for Dwight Schneider and the other for Kurt Schneider, or one for Dwight S. and the other for Kurt Schneider. For these profiles use real photos that naturally hide parts of your face or use photos in which your face is not the primary focus. After your alternate profile is completed, you can optionally start adding random people to your network so that it doesn't look weird that the profile has no connections, although you could always change the visibility options for those just as well. I do recommend adding people, though, as it makes the profile look more natural.

Don't be afraid of doing this—the chances of you getting "found out" by anyone that matters are slim to none. Recruiters are clueless—all they see is a name and CV keywords; they're not actively thinking the profile they're contacting is actually of someone they've already seen; they will take you at your word.

I once applied to the same company with different profiles and the same recruiter called me twice the same day—to the same phone number; once in the morning inquiring about one position, once in the evening asking about the second. He had no clue it was the same person. It's only logical; we don't easily remember random strings of numbers or names, and people are busy trying to fill quotas. People don't know what you know about your own context, that is, people have no clue your CV is "tweaked" or that you have plans to work multiple jobs at the same time—people have no idea what you're trying to pull. People don't usually go against the inertia of their own lives and work, as they have little incentive to do so. Job stacking goes *with* the inertia of all the regular processes companies and people in those companies have, so you have little to worry about. Understand that people don't care; they have their own work, their own personal problems, their own life to keep them busy. People are not against you and are not trying to figure out everything you might be doing or hiding. People are in it for themselves, so give them enough to get them going through their own processes and they'll hardly ever lift a finger to go the extra mile. So calm down, you'll be fine. I'll repeat: Nobody knows what you know about yourself and what you're doing, and more importantly, nobody cares to find out. Nobody notices, nobody cares, so feel free.

Appendix C Initiative drive

An initiative drive is where we temporarily disregard the rule or idea of not increasing your own visibility or responsibility at your job. Now why would we want to do something like this, after everything said in this book about how climbing the corporate ladder is nonsensical and how responsibility or ownership is pointless? Well, let's say you have found a job that fits your job-stacking goals (almost) perfectly: The position is fine, the company is high-trust and low in expectations, you're happy with it, but...maybe your team or your boss are not as trusting as you'd like, or maybe you have developed an unwanted reputation of being "distracted" or "lazy" that has temporarily decreased trust in you.

If you think about it, a reduction in trust is a kind of increase in visibility already—people are looking at you more because they don't trust you as much. So in this rare case we may want to simply do something that attracts visibility in a positive context and use that to ultimately lower visibility while we increase trust in general.

The idea is simple: temporarily show more engagement, less distraction, and be more willing to bear more responsibility. The best way to do this is to propose some sort of project or investigation that you can do (or lead) to help others or help some process within the company. Follow typical work advancement advice and identify an opportunity for your team or project to improve and simply propose a solution or project to implement that addresses that need for improvement.

Keep in mind that this is a "drive"; it's supposed to be short-lived. Don't go and get yourself into something permanent. You want to do something that has clear goals and dates. Don't over-extend and get yourself into something with which no one can know when or if you're actually done.

After it's over and you have the increased trust you like, lay off the gas.

APPENDIX D MANAGING TRACKING SOFTWARE

Tracking software is a clear sign of low trust and a bad company, so the first recommendation would be to try to find a better job. But that may be hard to do in some industries where the practice and use of tracking is widespread. Fortunately, if the jobs are remote, tracking software does not stop us from job stacking.

Companies use tracking software on their employees for a few reasons: to have leverage against you in case of some dispute; as a kind of quality assurance in the case that the company bills their clients by the hour; to give them "peace of mind." Sometimes the tracking is even requested by the company's clients and not the company itself. So the first thing you need to understand is that companies that use tracking software are not looking at anything specific most of the time and are not looking at any specific employee. Tracking software produces incredible amounts of information and noise that no company has the resources to sit through every day, week or month. Imagine a tracking software that takes a picture of your desktop every 10 minutes. That's 480 pictures for one day of work—now multiply that by whatever the amount of employees the company has is. No company can keep track of all of that, and if by some strange method they actually do, then quit. When I was stacking bad jobs that used tracking software I never got into any trouble or issue because of the tracking; no one ever said anything or came gave me a "concerned talk" about what the tracker was capturing. I was even able to see my "work log," and seeing that log, seeing the crazy amount of screenshots and stats, was when I realized no one could possibly be looking at this in any detail; not even I could tell at a glance what work was being done and I was the one that did it.

Companies that use tracking software can only keep track of simple stuff, like hours logged in, or at worst look for "patterns of behavior," so if the pattern of activity fits what is expected of the position and doesn't raise any red flags, they won't look further or into any details. So if you're remote, don't fear the tracker.

Now that you understand all of this, handling the trackers is quite simple: all you need to do is fool it into thinking you're actually working. Something as simple as moving your mouse every few minutes or typing stuff is enough. If the tracking includes taking screenshots, simply have appropriate content on your screen all the time. Do things like open a document and move it to different parts every few minutes so the pictures look different enough at a quick glance, and cycle through different software programs the company uses. If you do all of this while mixing in actual work from time to time, then no one will raise an eyebrow at your work activity. It really is that simple; most of the issues with tracking software as a job stacker are taken care of by having a computer for each job you have.

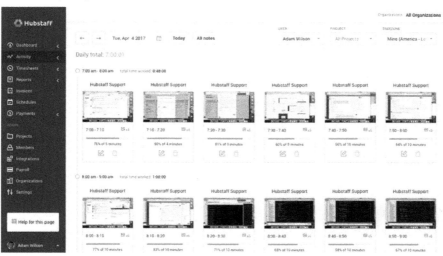

Hubstaff is a popular employee tracking application. This is what a couple of hours of activity look like in reports.
Image taken from https://www.cfncs.com.

CPSIA information can be obtained
at www.ICGtesting.com
Printed in the USA
BVHW091528150223
658293BV00020BA/2504